3. 8

1.0

BARRY
THE BRAVEST
SAINT BERNARD

by Lynn Hall
illustrated by Antonio Castro

A STEPPING STONE BOOK™
Random House 🏠 New York

Text copyright © 1973 by Lynn Hall. Illustrations copyright © 1992 by Antonio Castro. All rights reserved. Published in the United States by Random House Children's Books, a division of Random House, Inc., New York. Originally published by Touchwood Press in 1973. Subsequently published with different illustrations in 1992 by Random House, Inc. This is an abridgment of the 1992 Random House edition.

RANDOM HOUSE and colophon are registered trademarks and A STEPPING STONE BOOK and colophon are trademarks of Random House, Inc.

www.steppingstonesbooks.com
www.randomhouse.com/kids

Educators and librarians, for a variety of teaching tools, visit us at
www.randomhouse.com/teachers

Library of Congress Cataloging-in-Publication Data
Hall, Lynn.
Barry : the bravest Saint Bernard / by Lynn Hall ; illustrated by Antonio Castro.
— 1st Stepping Stone ed.
    p. cm.
ISBN 978-0-375-84439-3 (trade pbk.) — ISBN 978-0-375-94439-0 (lib. bdg.)
1. Barry (Dog)—Juvenile literature. 2. Saint Bernard dog—Switzerland—
Biography—Juvenile literature. [1. Barry (Dog). 2. Saint Bernard dog. 3. Dogs.]
I. Castro, Antonio, ill. II. Title.
SF429.S3H35 2007
636.73—dc22   2006100345

Printed in the United States of America   10 9 8 7 6 5 4 3 2 1

CONTENTS

1 - BARRY AND WERNER

The snow was pink from the setting sun.
Even the walls and windows of the stone
buildings looked pink.

Werner stepped out into the deep snow,
carrying a huge tub of dog food. He pulled
back the heavy door of the dogs' building.

"Dinner time!" he called.

The room inside was big and almost

bare. There were piles of straw against the walls. Now, from the straw came fourteen huge brown and white dogs.

The dogs pressed close, but they were gentle. They seemed to know how strong they were. Werner filled each of their dishes. Then he took the last dish, the biggest one, to a quiet corner of the room. One of the dogs followed him.

"There you are, Barry. I saved the best for you." Werner stood close to the giant animal.

Barry pushed his head up under Werner's chin and snuffled. He took the boy's arm in his huge jaws and shook it. Werner laughed.

The Saint Bernard Monastery, where the

dogs lived, was high in the mountains of
Switzerland. In those days there were no
cars or highways, only horses and mountain
trails. The only way over the mountains
was through the Saint Bernard pass.

The pass was named for the monastery,
a huge stone building where monks lived
and worked. The monks had a special kind

of work to do. They helped travelers going through the pass. In winter the snow was deep and dangerous. Sometimes people were buried under huge snow slides, or avalanches. Then the monks tried to find them and save them.

For this special work, the monks of the Saint Bernard Monastery had bred a wonderful kind of dog, which was also called a Saint Bernard. The dogs were big and powerful and could smell people trapped under the snow.

Werner loved all of the dogs at the monastery, but there was a special bond between him and Barry. They were both too young to help with the dangerous rescue work. Werner and Barry would have to wait until they were older.

The boy and the dog played roughly for a few minutes. Then Werner picked up the tub and started back toward the warm, bright monastery kitchen. His own supper would be ready by now. He was hungry for it.

But Father Benedict called to him. "Werner, come here, please."

Father Benedict was standing beside two steaming horses. The men who had been riding the horses stood nearby.

Werner put down the tub and walked toward them. Father Benedict said, "We have guests, Werner. Will you take their horses, please?"

Werner smiled at the two men. He took
their horses into the stable to make them
comfortable for the night. As he pulled the
saddle off one horse, the saddle bags hit his
arm. They were very heavy. Werner hung
the saddle on the side of the stall. Then he
lit a candle and opened one of the bags.

He thought, "If I were a monk, I couldn't snoop like this. I'm glad I'm not one, yet."

Inside the bag were a heavy pistol and a leather sack. From the shape of the sack, Werner was sure it was full of coins. His heart began to pound with fear.

The door blew open. Werner jumped. But it was only Father Benedict.

"Come here, Father," he called. He would have to admit that he had snooped.

Father Benedict came into the stall.

"Look," Werner said. "Those men are thieves! There's a gun in this bag, and a sack of gold. I know I shouldn't have looked, but . . ."

Father Benedict spoke calmly. "The doors of Saint Bernard are open to anyone who needs shelter."

"But, Father! They have a gun. They came to rob us."

The monk just smiled. He said, "We don't know that, do we? One of our guests asked for his bags. I'll take them. You go on inside before your supper gets cold." Father

Benedict took the saddle bags inside.

As Werner walked toward the lighted kitchen, he shook his head. Father Benedict's unfailing calm often puzzled the boy. The Father followed Werner into the kitchen.

The large, warm kitchen smelled of soup and onions. At the long table sat twelve monks and the two travelers. Werner sat at the far end, away from the strangers.

When the meal was over, one of the strangers stood up. In his hand was the gun!

"I thank you for the food," he said. "Now I'll thank you for your money."

Fearfully Werner looked at the gun. Then he looked at the monks across from him. Their faces were calm.

Father Benedict spoke. "We are a poor order. We have no money."

The robber laughed. "I know better than that. Everyone stand up and stay together."

The monks and Werner got up from the table. It seemed to Werner that he was the only one who was afraid.

Father Benedict said, "Very well. I see I can't fool you. Come this way."

He opened the door and went out into the yard. The monks, with Werner in the center, walked behind. The robbers followed the monks. With great dignity, Father Benedict moved toward the dogs' building. Werner was confused. There was no treasure in there, he knew. He opened his mouth to speak. The monk beside him poked him with his elbow.

At the door Father Benedict stopped. He stood aside. "All of our wealth is behind these doors," he said. "Gentlemen, help yourselves!"

The robbers ran forward and opened the heavy doors. Fourteen huge animals leaped out. Their mouths were open. Their teeth shone in the moonlight. Barry grabbed a robber's arm. He shook it and began to growl.

The robbers screamed as the dogs knocked the gun loose. The gun flew through the air. It landed softly in the snow. Still screaming, the men ran into the stable. A few seconds later, they came out riding their horses bareback. They disappeared into the darkness.

The monks laughed and went back to the bright, warm kitchen. Werner led the dogs into their building. He was grinning.

"Barry, you old robber-chaser, you really scared them. And I'm so glad!"

The dog growled and gently took Werner's wrist in his mouth. His tail wagged with happiness.

2 - TRAINING DAYS

The months passed, and soon summer
came. The mountains were so high that
even in summer it snowed nearly every
week, but the snow melted almost as it fell.
Flowers bloomed with snow on their petals.

The mountains were beautiful in summer.

Barry had his first birthday in June, and
his training began. Brother Luigi, the elderly
trainer, took Barry and the other young dogs
out every morning. They romped in the
snow for three hours. Werner went along to
watch and learn, and help when he could.

Werner's part in the training was to hide from the dogs. He would bury himself in the snow. Then he'd wait until one of the dogs found him and dug him up. All of the dogs were experts at smelling a human through the snow, but Barry's big nose seemed more remarkable than the others.

Almost always, it was Barry who found Werner first. The huge dog would dig away the snow. Then he would put his warm body close to Werner's and lick the boy's face. They both pretended Werner was freezing to death. Werner lay as still as he could while Barry's tongue tickled him. When he could stand it no longer, he began to giggle. Then Barry's tail wagged with joy.

When winter came, Barry was allowed
to go on real journeys along the pass. He
helped guide travelers and looked for people
who might be in trouble. An avalanche
could quickly bury anyone in its path. If
help didn't arrive in time, the victims would
freeze or smother from lack of air.

Every morning Barry went down the
mountain with Brother Luigi or one of the

other monks. There, beside the trail, was a stone hut. If there were travelers waiting in the hut, the dogs led them up the trail through the dangerous mountain pass. It was an all-day walk.

By the end of that winter, it was clear that Barry was the best rescue dog the monks had ever had. When an avalanche struck, Barry was the first to find people buried under the snow. He was the fastest to dig them out. Barry worked hardest to warm them up. Sometimes the other dogs gave up. But Barry would go on licking a frozen face until there was some movement. Then the great dog would go wild with joy.

3 - A TERRIBLE WINTER

Years passed. Werner grew tall and thin.
Now he gave all of his time to the dogs. He
worked with Brother Luigi every day. He fed
the dogs, played with them, and helped
train the pups. He was completely happy.

When Barry was six years old, Werner
was eighteen. That was the most terrible
winter the monks had known. Rescue trips

19

were made every day. Half of the monastery dogs died trying to save travelers. Many of the monks were lost in blizzards, too. Their own brave dogs could not save them.

One night in late March, Werner and Barry were walking slowly up the trail toward home. They were both tired and cold. It had been a terrible winter for them.

The sky was black. The mountain peaks could not be seen in the dark. Only a faint glow rose from the snow.

Suddenly there was a roar above them, like thunder. Werner and Barry both knew the sound, and dreaded it. Werner got down on his knees and pulled Barry close to him. The roar became a SWOOSH. A wall of

snow came down the mountainside, just
behind them.

When the night was still again, Werner
got up. His heart was pounding.

"That was too close, Barry," he said.
"We were almost killed. Let's get home and
let them know we're all right."

He walked on, but Barry did not follow. The dog stared up the mountainside. He was sniffing the air. He seemed confused.

"Is there someone up there? Go and find him," Werner said. But Barry stood still.

Werner was painfully cold. He was as tired as he had ever been in his life. "Come along, Barry," he ordered. He tried to pull the dog by the collar. Barry would not move his two hundred pounds.

For several minutes, Werner tried to get Barry to move one way or another. Barry just stood still in the same spot.

"All right, come on home when you're ready. You know the way." Werner moved up the trail toward the warmth of home.

The next morning, five of the monks set out to look for Barry. Werner took them back to the place where he had left Barry, but the dog was gone. The winds and the blowing snow had covered his tracks.

All day the monks searched, and all the next day. But they found no sign of Barry.

On the evening of the second day, Werner left the search party and went home. He had to take care of the other dogs. He must do his work, but he hated to give up looking for Barry. He had never felt so unhappy in his life. Barry was his best friend. Because Werner had left him, Barry was lost. He might very well be dead.

Werner went to the monastery kitchen

and mixed the huge tub of food for the dogs. As he went out the back door, he remembered all the nights he had fed Barry and played with him.

Suddenly he saw something in the shadows beside the stable. A dog with a large bundle on its back moved slowly out into the moonlight. Werner dropped the tub.

It was Barry.

"Father Benedict!" Werner shouted as loudly as he could. The call echoed back from the mountain peaks. "Benedict . . ."

A woman's shawl was tied around Barry's chest. Under the shawl Werner's hands found a child. It was a small boy.

From the monastery, Father Benedict

and the others came running. They breathed
into the boy's mouth. They rubbed him with
snow to make his blood move faster through
his body. He moved, cried out.

Werner led Barry into the dogs'
building. Gently he fed Barry. The great dog
was so tired he could barely chew. When he
stretched out on the straw to sleep, his head

was in Werner's lap. His jaws gently held Werner's arm.

It was several days before the body of the child's mother was found. When Barry had found her and her son, she was very weak. She was just able to tie the boy onto Barry's back with her shawl before she died.

Three years later, Brother Luigi was lost during a rescue trip. When he did not come home, Father Benedict opened the kennel door and told Barry, "Find your master."

Barry found him, buried under tons of snow. The great dog worked harder than he had ever worked before, but it was too late. Luigi was dead. Sadly, Werner took over the trainer's duties.

4 - ONE LAST RESCUE

Three years passed. It was October, and
the day had been crisply cool. But as night
came, the first heavy snow of the year
began to fall.

In the monastery kitchen, three old
friends sat enjoying the fire and the company
of one another. Father Benedict and Werner
sat close to the fireplace. Barry lay nearby.

28

Werner had become a monk, and he was now a young man of twenty-four. He moved his foot and rubbed the toe of his shoe against Barry's hip. The dog's eyes stayed closed, but his tail thumped the floor. He rolled over onto his back so Werner's foot could rub under his ribs.

The dark spots on Barry's head now showed some white hairs. His back sagged slightly with age when he walked. But when the monastery dogs were let out each morning for their run in the snow, Barry still bounded with them.

It had been still in the kitchen for several minutes when Werner said, "I'm being selfish, am I not?"

Father Benedict didn't need to ask what
Werner meant. "It isn't easy to give up a
friend like Barry," the Father said gently.

"Still, this must be his last year," Werner

said. "The winters are too cold up here for an old dog. I think we may not use him this winter for rescue work. We'll let him stay here, just for company. Then next summer, when we take the puppies down to the city to be sold, Barry can go along. Our friends will keep him there, and he can rest in a warmer place. He has earned that."

The Father smiled down at the sleeping dog. "Yes, Barry has been the greatest of all our dogs. There may never be another rescue dog who works with the devotion of this old fellow. Barry has saved forty lives all by himself. It is indeed a fine record."

"I hope this summer's pups will—" Werner was interrupted by the sound of the knocker at the front door. He and the Father exchanged glances—it was late for travelers. The two men moved through the long stone hallway. The yawning, wagging Barry followed them sleepily.

Werner opened the door.

A shivering boy was standing on the steps.

"Come inside," Werner said.

In the kitchen, the monks stirred up the fire. They set a pot of soup on to boil.

When the boy was able to talk, he said, "I thank you for your kindness. My brother Martin was called to serve in the army, and didn't want to go. So he ran away from

home three days ago. He took only his jacket, a loaf of bread, and a knife to cut it with. Our mother told me to come and ask you to look for him." The boy's eyes were shining with tears, which he tried to hide.

Father Benedict said, "Do you know which way he went?"

Werner had already left to call the other monks and wake up the dogs.

Within minutes the search party was on its way—eight monks and six dogs. Werner had shut Barry in the kitchen, but before the party had reached the trail, the old dog found an open door. He raced to join Werner.

A full moon lighted the night. The snow

had stopped falling. Trees, rocks, monks, and dogs were black against the pale gray snow. The group moved down the mountainside to a place the boy had named. Then they separated, monks and dogs

spreading out to cover the area. Each monk carried a long stick to poke into the snow in case an avalanche had buried young Martin.

Barry and Werner moved lower on the mountain slope than the others. Most of

Werner's mind was on the job of finding Martin. A part of it was thinking that this would probably be the last time he followed Barry through the mountains they both loved.

There had been hundreds of dogs in Werner's care these past years. Many were Barry's sons and daughters. All were fine dogs; each was lovable in his own way. But none had the deep wisdom that shone in Barry's eyes. None could equal the great old dog's ability to save human lives. No other dog had ever meant so much to Werner.

The two of them were alone on the slope. Barry moved ahead, his nose near the snow.

Suddenly he stopped. He raised his huge

head and swung it slowly from side to side. Then he galloped down the hillside behind a clump of pine trees. Werner called to the others and started after Barry.

Suddenly there was a scream. "BEAR!"

Werner rounded the trees and stopped. A young man held tightly to a tree. His eyes were wide and staring. In his hand was a knife, red with blood. At his feet lay Barry.

For the first time in his life, Werner paid no attention to the human. He knelt over Barry, whose side and neck were bleeding.

An hour later, both Barry and Martin had been carried on stretchers to the monastery. The boy was asleep in the warmest of the guest rooms, with his young brother watching over him.

Barry lay still on a bed of soft blankets near the kitchen fire while Werner cleaned and bandaged his wounds. Around him stood a ring of silent, worried friends.

"He's a very old dog," the Father said softly. "To lose that much blood . . ."

"He will get well." Werner's jaw was shut so hard the words could barely get out.

The Father put a hand on Werner's shoulder. "I hope you don't blame the boy. He was out of his head with cold and fear. Barry came leaping toward him in the moonlight. It was natural enough that he should mistake Barry for a bear. The lad was probably afraid of wild animals, too."

"I know," Werner sighed. "Of course I don't blame him. But I wonder what Barry must have thought. He went forth with love and was stabbed for it."

All night and all the next day, Barry lay

without moving. Werner sat for long hours with the old dog's head in his lap. Finally, on the evening of the second day, Barry stirred. His eyes opened. His tail moved against the bedding. He opened his mouth and closed it, weakly, around Werner's arm.

By morning, he was able to drink a little water and eat some food. That night, it was clear that the dog was not yet ready to die. The ancient stone walls of the Saint Bernard Monastery echoed with joy.

Two years later, after a peaceful retirement in the village, Barry died of old age. His body is now on display in a Swiss museum.

It was a hundred years after his death

before the Saint Bernard monks had another dog great enough to be named Barry. Since that time, it has become a tradition to give the honored name of Barry to the finest dog at the monastery.

There is a Barry there today.